TROODON

ODON

The Smartest Dinosaur

by Don Lessem

illustrations by Donna Braginetz

 Carolrhoda Books Inc./Minneapolis

Special thanks to Dr. Philip J. Currie, Head of
Dinosaur Research, Royal Tyrrell Museum of
Paleontology, for his invaluable help in the
preparation of this book.

Carolrhoda Books, Inc. c / o The Lerner Group
241 First Avenue North, Minneapolis, MN 55401

Lessem, Don.
    Troodon, the smartest dinosaur / by Don Lessem ;
illustrations by Donna Braginetz.
        p. cm. — (Special dinosaurs)
    Includes index.
    Summary : Describes the research and paleontological
investigation that led to the identification and classification
of the dinosaur Troodon.
    ISBN 0-87614-798-8
    1. Troodon—Juvenile literature. [1. Troodon. 2.
Dinosaurs. 3. Paleontology. 4. Fossils.] I. Braginetz,
Donna, ill. II. Title. III. Series.
QE862.S3L47 1996
567.9'7—dc20   92-44689
                                                      CIP
                                                      AC

Manufactured in the United States of America
1 2 3 4 5 6 - I/JR - 00 99 98 97 96 95

To Marvin Levy, a good friend to me and dinosaurs—D.L.
To Mom and Dad—D.B.

Opposite page: A group of *Troodon* wait to attack their prey, an *Orodromeus.*

The setting sun glows orange over a warm and humid riverbank. Along the green shore, a little dinosaur munches on a fern. From far away, a pack of keen-eyed hunting dinosaurs spots the single animal. The hunters dash in silently on long hind legs and surround the little dinosaur. Baring their sharp teeth, they seize their **prey**.

These hunters aren't much bigger than adult humans. Yet they are among the deadliest of dinosaur killers because they are smart. The predators are *Troodon* (TRO-uh-don), and scientists think that they are the smartest of all dinosaurs.

How we came to know about *Troodon* and its intelligence is a story of human reasoning, hard work, and good luck.

For many years, people thought that all dinosaurs were stupid creatures. That's because the dinosaurs that we knew best had remarkably tiny brains. The plate-backed *Stegosaurus*, as big as a tank, had a brain the size of a walnut. The brain of the giant dinosaur *Apatosaurus*, one of the biggest animals ever to walk the earth, was as small as the brain of a horse.

You can't always judge the intelligence of an animal by the size of its brain. But big brains and intelligence do often go together. Humans, apes, and dolphins have the biggest brains of all animals, compared to their body size. And we know that these animals, especially humans, can learn and perform other mental activities beyond the reach of small-brained animals like snakes.

The brain does many different jobs in the body. It controls not only thought and memory but also an animal's movements and what it senses of its surroundings. Bigger-brained animals usually have sharper senses than smaller-brained ones. They can often move more quickly. And bigger-brained animals can learn more complicated behaviors, from hunting together to communicating with each other.

From what we know about brain size and intelligence, we are probably safe in saying that the giant dinosaurs with tiny brains weren't very smart, at least compared to humans. But not all dinosaurs were pea-brains. **Paleontologists** (pay-lee-on-TAHL-uh-jists)—scientists who study dinosaurs—have discovered that they were a tremendously varied group of animals. We now know about more than 300 different kinds of dinosaurs. And our knowledge is growing very fast; a new dinosaur is discovered about every 7 weeks. People have been digging up dinosaurs for nearly 200 years, but about half of all dinosaurs we know have been found in the last 20 years.

Above: Apatosaurus was more than ten times bigger than a modern-day horse, but its skull was only a few inches bigger. These illustrations show the overall size of both animals compared to each other, and the relative sizes of their brains.

Brachiosaurus
(82 feet long, 52 feet tall)

Tyrannosaurus
(40 feet long)

Plateosaurus
(27½ feet long)

Adult human
(5½ feet tall)

Compsognathus
(3⅓ feet long)

We should not be surprised to learn that dinosaurs were different. Dinosaurs lived on earth for 160 million years. During this vast period of time, dinosaurs inhabited widely different places around the world. Some made their homes in swamps. Others lived in deserts and in cold polar climates.

Dinosaurs were also very different in size. Some were no bigger than chickens, while others were as tall as five-story office buildings. And dinosaurs also differed in their intelligence.

The huge, pea-brained dinosaurs like *Apatosaurus* probably didn't need to be smart. Their way of life may not have included activities that depended on a large brain. But recent discoveries have shown that some dinosaurs were capable of doing things like running fast, seeing well, or protecting their herds that might have required a lot of brain power.

Dinosaurs came in a wide range of sizes. Some were many times bigger than an average human.

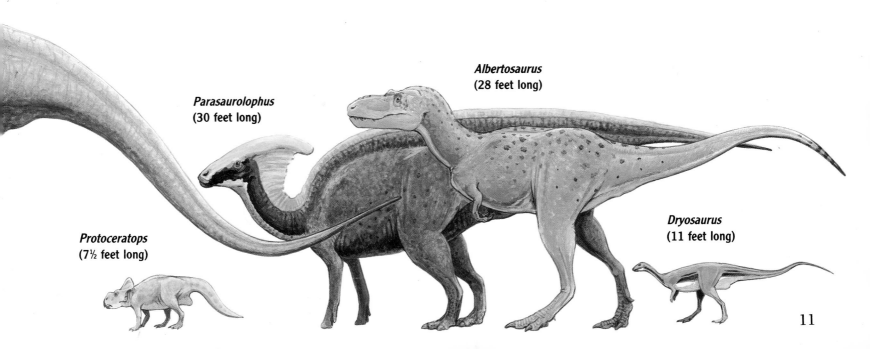

Albertosaurus
(28 feet long)

Parasaurolophus
(30 feet long)

Dryosaurus
(11 feet long)

Protoceratops
(7½ feet long)

11

By measuring the spacing of footprints, we know that some dinosaur hunters could run as fast as 25 miles an hour. Footprints left by certain **herbivorous** (er-BIH-vuh-ruhs), or plant-eating, dinosaurs show that these animals traveled in herds, protecting their young in the middle of the group. Skulls of dinosaurs found in Australia have huge eye sockets. In dinosaur times, Australia was near the South Pole, and it was dark there for many weeks of the year. These dinosaurs probably had large eyes to help them see.

A large-eyed animal needs a large brain to receive and understand the messages picked up by its eyes. Animals that are active hunters or cooperate in taking care of their young would also need big brains. Their intelligence would have to be greater than that of reptiles and many other kinds of animals.

This kind of evidence suggests that not all dinosaurs were stupid. Studying the brain sizes of dinosaurs can provide more evidence. But how do you measure the brain of an animal that has been dead for at least 65 million years?

eye socket

The top of the skull of a hypsilophodont found in Australia. Like *Troodon,* this dinosaur had large eye sockets.

Some fossilized dinosaur parts: the skull and jaws of a *Stegoceras*, and some skin from an *Edmontosaurus*.

Paleontologists learn about dinosaurs' brains in the same way that they learn about other parts of dinosaurs—by studying **fossils.** It takes special circumstances to make a fossil, which is why it isn't easy to find dinosaur fossils. To become fossilized, an animal's body must be covered by mud or sand soon after the animal dies. If the body remains covered, minerals can enter into the bones and harden and preserve them. They become fossils.

Almost any bony part of an animal can be turned into a fossil. We have fossil dinosaur teeth, claws, and armor. Sometimes we even find fossilized impressions of dinosaur skin. But the **soft tissue** inside a dinosaur's body, including the brain, very rarely becomes fossilized. These soft body parts decay too quickly.

13

A fossilized *Troodon* braincase found in Alberta, Canada, in 1982, seen from the side. The large opening is the dinosaur's eye socket.

But there is a way to estimate how large a dinosaur's brain was. To do this, we need to find its fossilized **braincase,** the bony cup that holds the brain in the skull. Paleontologists measure the braincase and figure out the size of the brain that would fit into it. Then they can compare the fossil animal's brain and body size to the brains and body sizes of living animals. From that comparison, the scientists can make some good guesses about how smart the animal was.

Of all the dinosaurs we know, *Troodon* had the biggest braincase compared to its body size. This tells us that *Troodon* had the biggest brain of all known dinosaurs and was probably the smartest.

It was only through a combination of lucky accidents that scientists learned about *Troodon* and its big brain. *Troodon* fossils were first found in 1856 by Joseph Leidy, a scientist from Philadelphia. What Dr. Leidy discovered were just a few sharp teeth. He wasn't sure if they belonged to a dinosaur, a lizard, or some other kind of animal. He named the mysterious creature *Troodon,* which means "wounding tooth."

Dr. Joseph Leidy, shown with the legbone of a *Hadrosaurus.*

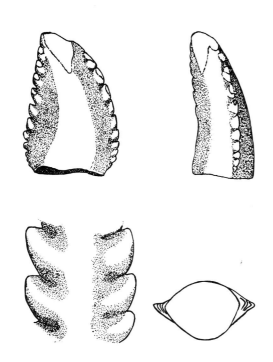

Above: Four drawings of a *Troodon* tooth from the front of the upper jaw, showing the serrations (top left and right), a back view of the tooth (bottom left), and a cross-section (bottom right). *Below:* Two *Orodromeus*, a type of hypsilophodont. Scientists once thought *Troodon* was also a hypsilophodont.

For many years after *Troodon* was named, scientists were uncertain about the identity of the animal that had those sharp little teeth. Whatever kind of animal it was, *Troodon* was a **carnivore** (KAR-nih-vor), or meat-eater. Its teeth were **serrated** (suh-RAYT-id), with notched edges like those on a steak knife.

Serrated teeth would have helped *Troodon* saw through flesh. Other predators have these kind of teeth. But the narrowness of *Troodon's* teeth near their roots made them different from the teeth of any known meat-eating dinosaur.

For more than a century, *Troodon* remained a mystery. Then, in 1978, paleontologist John R. "Jack" Horner found many *Troodon* teeth in western Montana. The teeth were scattered among the skeletons of little plant-eating dinosaurs called **hypsilophodonts** (hip-so-LOF-uh-donts). So Dr. Horner decided that *Troodon* must have been a member of this dinosaur group, even though some of its teeth were like those of a meat-eater. Perhaps if more *Troodon* teeth or even a whole jaw were found, the animal might turn out to have other teeth more like those we know from plant-eating hypsilophodonts.

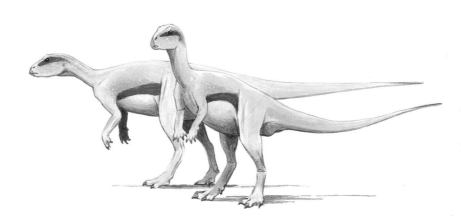

Dr. Horner is one of the world's leading paleontologists and an expert at finding fossils. But when he did discover more *Troodon* fossils, he found out that he had been wrong about what kind of animal *Troodon* was.

One day in 1983, Dr. Horner drove 400 miles to the city of Drumheller in Alberta, Canada. He went to visit his friend Dr. Philip Currie, another paleontologist. Phil Currie is an expert on the teeth of meat-eating dinosaurs.

Drs. Horner and Currie went for a walk in the badlands near the building site of the new Royal Tyrrell Museum, one of the world's largest museums of fossils. Badlands are areas of barren hills and valleys.

Most of the plants and soil have been stripped away by blustery winds and dry air, exposing rock from ancient times. Because this old rock is out in the open, badlands are excellent places to look for fossils that might have formed long ago.

Dr. Currie and Dr. Horner walked the badlands near Drumheller with their heads down, searching for fossils. Soon Dr. Horner spotted a small piece of bone lying on the ground. He examined it closely and saw part of a jaw with some teeth still in it. Horner showed the teeth to Dr. Currie, who recognized them as *Troodon's*. The rest of the jaw could be seen sticking out of the hillside.

Technicians on a dig in northwestern China using tools to remove a dinosaur fossil from the ground. Removing fossils is a delicate and time-consuming process.

Before scientists remove a delicate fossil from the ground, they have a lot of work to do. Dirt must be carefully removed from the bone with small tools. The fossil must be coated with preservatives to harden it. The location of the fossil must be mapped to help determine how the animal died and how its bones became fossilized. Phil Currie decided that he would return to the site the next day with his field crew to carefully **excavate** (EK-skuh-vait) the *Troodon* jawbone.

But the next morning, it rained so heavily that the crew could not go out. The rains continued for a week. By the time that Dr. Currie could go back and look for the jawbone, mud had covered it over. He could no longer find the one-of-a-kind fossil. Knowing that he had seen, and then lost, the evidence he needed to figure out more about the mysterious *Troodon*, Phil Currie felt extremely frustrated. For days he hunted for the missing jawbone before abandoning his search.

Then, in 1985, Dr. Horner returned to Drumheller to visit Dr. Currie. Once again, they went on a fossil-hunting walk in the badlands behind the museum. Looking down, Jack Horner saw something amazing. It was the same *Troodon* jawbone he had spotted two years earlier! The discovery was as lucky as finding a needle in a haystack—twice. This time, Dr. Horner and Dr. Currie put an orange flag in the ground beside the fossil to mark the find.

Dr. Currie and his crew dug up the jawbone and took it to the laboratory for cleaning and preparing. Cleaning fossils is difficult, delicate work. Rock is scraped from bones using dentist's tools and little air-powered drills equipped with needle-sharp tips. It can take months, even years, to clean a fossil. But the results can be very revealing to a scientist.

A technician very carefully cleans the dirt from fossilized dinosaur eggs.

19

When Dr. Currie examined the clean jaw of *Troodon* under a microscope, he saw something very strange. The dinosaur had several different kinds of teeth in its mouth. Other known dinosaurs had teeth of only one shape. Some of *Troodon's* pointiest teeth looked like those that scientists had found on small predators. Other, thicker teeth were similar to the teeth of bigger meat-eating dinosaurs. But none of the teeth was anything like the teeth of the plant-eating hypsilophodont dinosaurs—the group to which Jack Horner thought that *Troodon* might belong.

Dr. Horner had been confused by finding *Troodon* teeth among the bones of hypsilophodonts. These plant-eaters were probably *Troodon's* prey, not its relatives. The teeth may have broken off when *Troodon* dinosaurs attacked a nest of young hypsilophodonts.

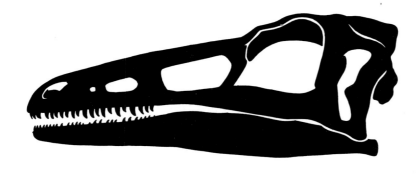

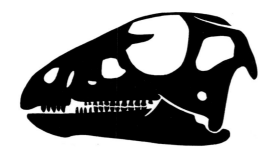

Left: As you can see from these illustrations, the teeth and skull of a typical *Troodon* (top) were very different from those of a typical hypsilophodont. *Opposite page:* Troodon attacking a nest of newly hatched hypsilophodonts.

When it roamed the earth 70 million years ago, *Troodon* was probably a hunter. Dr. Currie discovered just how smart a hunter *Troodon* might have been in 1986, the year after he and Jack Horner found the missing jawbone. It was in that year that Dr. Currie worked on a project with some paleontologists from China.

China has many dinosaur fossils, including some from the end of the dinosaur era, 80 million to 65 million years ago. During this period, the land masses of Asia and North America were connected in the arctic region. Now the two continents are separated by the Bering Sea, but in dinosaur times, animals could move back and forth between them. Because of this connection, many of the same dinosaurs lived in Asia and in western North America.

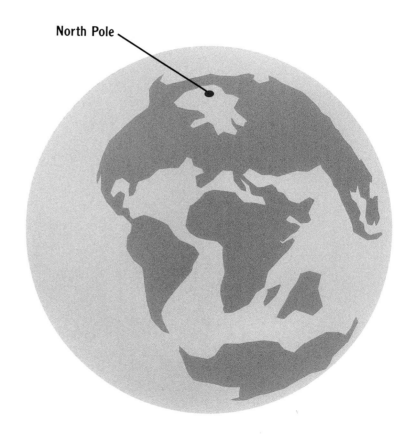

North Pole

This map shows how the Earth probably looked about 70 million years ago, when *Troodon* lived. North America and Asia were connected at the time.

Tang Zhilu near the spot in Alberta, Canada, where he found the *Troodon* braincase.

In 1986, the Chinese paleontologists came to Canada to compare North American dinosaurs to Asian ones from rocks of the same age. With Dr. Currie and other Canadian scientists, they went digging in an area called Dinosaur Park, not far from the Tyrrell Museum. During their excavation, a Chinese worker named Tang Zhilu spotted the curved pieces of a dinosaur's skull lying on the barren ground. From the size and shape of the pieces and some teeth found nearby, Dr. Currie identified Mr. Tang's discovery as the braincase of a *Troodon*.

In the Tyrrell Museum laboratory, Phil Currie pieced together the cleaned skull bones. They formed a case with an opening in it about the size of a small avocado. This opening once held *Troodon's* brain.

23

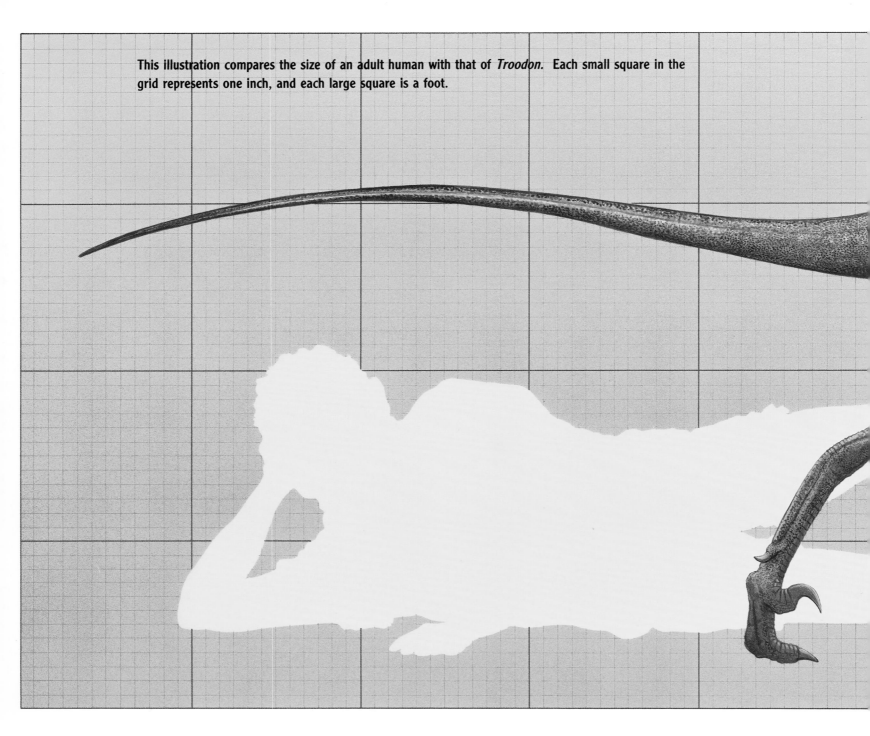

This illustration compares the size of an adult human with that of *Troodon*. Each small square in the grid represents one inch, and each large square is a foot.

An avocado might not seem very large for the size of an animal's brain. But it is large in relation to the size of *Troodon's* body. *Troodon* was a small dinosaur. Based on its jaw size, it wasn't much bigger than an adult human. No other dinosaur this small had a brain anywhere near as big as an avocado.

In proportion to its body size, *Troodon* had a bigger brain than any other known dinosaur, or any mammal, bird, fish, or reptile from dinosaur times. Its brain was even bigger than the brains of modern reptiles and of many birds alive today. *Troodon* was probably smarter than all these animals.

Why would *Troodon* have needed a big brain? Before paleontologists could answer this question, they had to know more about the dinosaur. Fortunately, after more than 100 years of finding no *Troodon* bones, scientists began finding a lot of them.

The Chinese paleontologists who visited Canada in 1986 invited Dr. Currie and other Canadian scientists to dig for Chinese dinosaurs. In the Gobi Desert of Inner Mongolia, the Chinese and Canadians found the delicate hand and arm bones of a close cousin of *Troodon*. Elsewhere in China, scientists found complete skeletons of dinosaurs that belonged to *Troodon's* family.

The best specimens of *Troodon* itself were discovered in the late 1980s by Jack Horner and his crew in Montana. They found fossilized *Troodon* eggs, 4 inches long and with pebbly shells. One of the eggs still had the bones of a tiny embryo inside. The Montana scientists also found three skeletons of *Troodon,* including a 2-foot-long youngster and others nearly 6 feet long.

This new evidence indicated that *Troodon* was a little dinosaur with large eyes. It had the long, curved legbones of a fast runner and front claws equipped to grip objects. With the help of this information, scientists could make some guesses about how *Troodon* might have used its big brain. It may have needed a large brain to control its body when running quickly. Brain power might also have been needed to work its gripping fingers or to provide a good sense of vision.

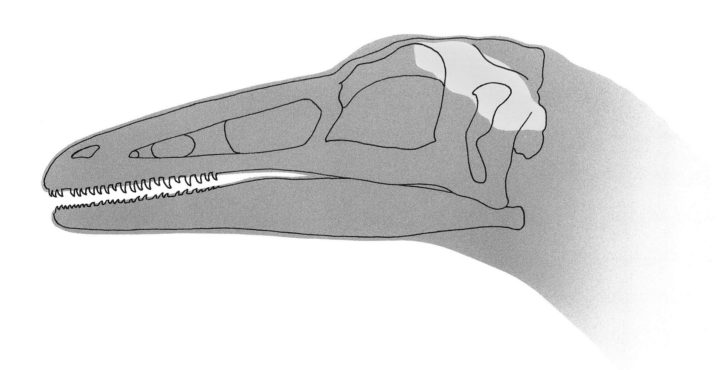

These are all guesses about *Troodon's* abilities. But the same guesswork seems to fit the dinosaurs that had brains almost as big as *Troodon's*. These are the fast-running **ornithomimid** (or-nih-tho-MY-mid) dinosaurs of Asia and North America and the big-eyed hypsilophodonts of Australia. Like *Troodon,* the ostrich-like ornithomimids could have used their big brains to run fast. And big brains would have helped Australian hypsilophodonts to see well and survive in the dark region near the South Pole.

From the physical features of *Troodon* and these other dinosaurs, we can get some idea of how the animals might have used their large brains. But we don't know how *Troodon* actually lived. Phil Currie thinks that *Troodon* may have been smart enough to do something pretty complicated—hunt in packs.

Many animals today team up to hunt for their food. Wolves hunt together, following a leader and circling their prey before attacking. Working together, they can kill a moose much larger than any one wolf. Wild dogs also hunt in a pack, and so do female lions. Even some lizards hunt in groups. Many people who live in the wilderness still get their food by hunting together.

Such cooperative hunting is possible only when animals are intelligent. Hunters must be able to outmaneuver and outsmart their prey. They also need to communicate with each other while hunting. Long swift legs, sharp teeth, and keen eyes are a predator's basic tools. But to make good use of its tools, a predator requires a powerful brain. *Troodon* had such a brain.

Above: Ornithomimid dinosaurs like these *Struthiomimus* had brains nearly as big as *Troodon's*. *Opposite page:* Scientists think *Troodon* may have hunted in packs.

However *Troodon* made its living, it survived for a long time. From the fossil evidence we have, it seems that few varieties of dinosaurs existed for more than a few million years. But some fossils discovered in China look very much like *Troodon,* and they are nearly 130 million years old. This is more than 50 million years older than the *Troodon* fossils from Canada and Montana.

Paleontologists were very surprised by the long history of *Troodon*-like dinosaurs. Perhaps *Troodon* and its relatives lasted so long because of their intelligence. This feature would have helped the animals to survive during difficult times. In fact, *Troodon* survived until the very end of the dinosaur era, about 65 million years ago. It was one of the last dinosaurs to become extinct.

Like *Troodon,* we humans are the smartest animals of our day. Humankind has been on Earth for about 1.5 million years so far, a small part of *Troodon's* time on the planet. If we're lucky as well as smart, maybe we can last as long as the smartest dinosaur.

Glossary

braincase: the bony structure that holds an animal's brain within its skull

carnivore: an animal that lives on a diet of meat

embryo: the developing young of an animal before birth

excavate: to dig out of the earth

fossils: the remains of a formerly living thing or its parts, preserved in rock or soil

herbivorous: living on a diet of plants

hypsilophodonts: a group of fast-running, plant-eating dinosaurs

ornithomimids: a group of dinosaurs that once lived in Asia and North America and are thought to have had relatively large brains

paleontologists: scientists who study the life forms of ancient times, using fossilized remains

predators: animals that hunt and kill other animals for food

prey: animals that are hunted and killed for food by other animals

serrated: having a notched, jagged edge, like the blade of a saw or bread knife

soft tissue: the inner parts of an animal's body

Photo Acknowledgments:

Photographs are reproduced through the courtesy of: Tom Rich, p. 12; Donald Baird, pp. 13 (both), 15; Royal Tyrrell Museum of Paleontology/Alberta Culture and Multiculturalism, pp. 14, 23, 26; Phillip Currie, p. 16; © The Ex Terra Foundation, pp. 17, 18, 19.

Index